SUFFER THE LITTLE VOICES

POEMS BY NATHAN BROWN

GREYSTONE PRESS
2220 N. E. 131st Street
Edmond, Oklahoma 73013

Library of Congress Cataloging-in-Publication Data
Poetry

Library of Congress Catalog Number
2005936416

ISBN: 0-9774576-1-3   Softcover: alk. paper

Cover by Chris Everett
Book design by Mia Blake

Other books by Nathan Brown
Hobson's Choice
Ashes Over The Southwest

GREYSTONE PRESS
2220 N. E. 131st Street
Edmond, Oklahoma 73013
2005

ACKNOWLEDGEMENTS

To Dr. Gladys Lewis: thank you so much for your love, support, and belief in me, and this book.

To Professor Robert Con Davis-Undiano: who oversaw many of these poems through the dissertation process and not only accepted the spirituality, but embraced it as well. Thank you so much, RC.

- - - - - - - -

Thanks to *Billy Crockett* for the ongoing conversation at Blue Rock, and anywhere else we happen to find ourselves.

Thanks to Chris Everett for your friendship and such beautiful covers for my books. This book, in particular, is a shared journey between us.

As always, I would like to thank my parents, Lavonn and Norma Brown. You encouraged me for quite some time to gather together the poems that hover around my struggle with religion and faith. You've even tolerated the ones you don't like.

- - - - - - - -

Special thanks to Sierra – my daughter: First—thank you so much for all your help in preparing this manuscript. I couldn't have done it without you. Honey, it's been a rough road for us. But I want you to know I will always love you more than anything else that lives and breathes on this planet.

for
Sierra

TABLE OF CONTENTS

SUFFER THE LITTLE VOICES

I.

This Time the Angel

Stunned,
I go for a walk.

For bigger conundrums
the pond is a good friend.

Half way round,
that shadow again,
the Great Blue Heron,
absent since the last visitation
and never before in daylight,
stands silently on the shore.

I wonder when she'll fly this time.
How close will she let me get?

Strangely   she stays,
watches cautiously.

And I know
I can't fly away either
as I've done in the past.

In Numbers, Chapter 22—
the angel is an ass.
A funny thing
for an angel to be.
But I'm one to talk…
This time the angel
is a Great Blue Heron.

Eyeless and Earless

The altar candle
drones on Sundays

a light the presbyters seek
but, theologically, are not
allowed to find—

a truth the elm limb knows
as it scrapes a white path
in the burning brick outside
a summer-laden church.

Back inside,
yawning glances
at a slow clock reveal
another more awkward truth—

a laughing, sideways truth
that feels no need to moralize
the hilarious sadness
in these pews.

A Month of Sunday

I.

It starts with the agitated beep
of my alarm clock, angry I'd set it
for such a ridiculous hour.

Then the wrestling match—
do I care enough to shower,
or should I just wash hair?
In the mirror I think
It's not all that bad as is... then,
Damn, I forgot to shave last night.

Now I'm in a hurry.
A "cereal only" kind of hurry.
A "cereal in the closet" kind of hurry.

Did I wear that last week?
I don't remember. I don't care.
I take a bite, set the bowl down.

Shoes tied, bowl to sink, keys in pocket,
guitar cases packed, I lock door,
go from door to car, *Do I have it all?*

II.

Quick setup and sound check,
then lead the acoustic praise and
worship at the first church—

always with the eyes closed because
I want to seem sincere, but actually
can't bear the thought of what I'm doing.

But they pay me well enough.

Next—I quickly tear down
and move on to the next church.

Here it's electric guitar and background
vocals—a little more fun. I keep my
eyes open, looking for a date.

But the last thing I want
is a good little Baptist girl
full of relentless Baptist guilt.

So, I quickly tear down again,
grab the box of leftover donuts,
head back to the house thinking:

I should go to the main service,
because the pastor is a friend
and I hurt for how he has to

baby-sit Christians in this playhouse,
when he'd rather be with sinners
he knows live closer to God.

III.

I go home anyway and begin
the ceremonial removal
of corduroy and put on the priestly

garments of cotton sweatpants
and school paraphernalia while
firing up the tubes on the altar.

Today's offering—Rams vs. Bears.
I prepare a sacrifice of wine in dancing

sunrays at play on the floor of my

sanctuary. Will God be pleased?
Is God ever pleased? Depends…
on whether your pastor is pleased or

pissed with the world around him,
the wife God's "given" him, and his
children he believes aren't drug dealers.

Depends on whether he believes terrorism
is an unfortunate side-effect, or the tool
of a God who hates fags and abortion doctors.

IV.

I lose my ability to care as I don the cleats and
slider pants of The Church of the Blue Dome
and feel my blood rising to the occasion.

Windows down, the sunroof back,
I drive slowly—extending the sacred
passage—to the Ultimate Frisbee field.

I arrive to the smiles and waves of the lost—
sacred, obscene gestures of deep friendship.
A love the church could never understand.

I spread the communion donuts before
my fellow church members, not a saint
among them, and we give thanks.

We hit the field, run until muscles pull,
smash into the ground, and then,
leaping up into blue, I feel the crash

of forgiven limbs and torsos, and
jump up, grass in mouth, dazed…
gazing into the face of God.

Soul-Savers

I gaze back at the pain and
disdain we felt for "the lost"
in covert planning sessions
we called Bible studies. Then

I turn my head away with a jerk
from the sight of my old church
in a weak and strained attempt
to push down this past stupidity—

a stupidity constructed through
millenniums of bad dogma,
which was "not busy livin'…
just busy dyin'," as Bob Dylan,

a theologian of a different cut,
tried to tell us in the years
we couldn't look past his
prophetic, soul-felt addictions.

My sighs and shaking head
signify the inevitable departure
from that, from them, not Jesus
[still my favorite hippie socialist

and, yes, Son of God].
But, I do realize, I'm afraid,
that in the nouns and verbs
I now choose to express myself,

I've certainly lost them,
the "they" I once was.
And I'm struck with the fear
that *now*… it's *me* they're after.

A Growing Concern

I'm a bit jaded. But
I still tear up every time Linus,
haloed in light, tells Charlie Brown
what Christmas is all about
from that empty school stage.

I admit my cynicism. But
I still pull my blanket up
to wipe my eyes when the bell rings
at the end of *It's a Wonderful Life*.
The little girl makes her proclamation.
Jimmy Stewart smiles up at Clarence.

I often agree with Goethe and Chekov
when they sing of the stupid masses.
But lately, I put my hand over my heart,
sing the national anthem at football games.

And I flat out cry when my daughter
wraps her porcelain arms around the left
pant leg of my jeans and looks up
with blazing blue-gray eyes still void
of all the shadows and doubts that eat
away at mine, and I find myself slapping
at a creeping, irrepressible urge
to hope.

Holy Days

Most of my offhanded holiday poems
hover over the prodigal family's return
at Thanksgiving, for some reason.

I would say it's because Christmas
and Easter are a bit too sacred
for the eye-poking darts of a poet.

But it's not like Christmas hasn't been effaced
by long term exposure to the red, green and gold
options from Victoria's Secret barelywear,

or a drunken Santa Claus stumbling
out of the giving zone onto 52nd Street.
It's just that the baby in a manger still has

the power to silence angry cities on the eve
of his celebrated birth, in spite of our vain
efforts to tie him up in lacey bows and ribbons.

And Easter, well… all the pink bunnies
and yellow eggs in the world haven't
been able to shake off the truth about

death—the necessity of it—the power,
and how it ultimately leads to forgiveness.
Poems cover this topic like snow in Siberia.

I wrote a poem about May Day once.
But that was about ripping scripture
out of context, and crosses doin' wheelies.

I wrote a poem about Labor Day once.
But that was mainly about Mexicans hammering
out the Anglo-American dream of subdivisions.

Maybe it's because Thanksgiving rides on the backs
of flapping black coats and big, dorky hats
with belt buckles above the brims, the costume

of brow-scrunched Puritans who came to save
the indigenous with the Tryptophan of dogma.
One of the faces of religion I don't mind slapping.

saviors

Seven, maybe
eight years old,
she struggles
with the drawstring
of funky jeans,
chin on her chest
in frustrated concentration.

Fortyish,
give or take,
he walks up
and around from behind,
jeans and red baseball hat,
kind eyes and soft
knowing smile,
he kneels down to help.

She's not embarrassed,
because he knows
just what to say.
She smiles.
Jesus weeps.

He scratches her brown hair
as he stands up.
They walk away,
two Christmas ribbons
silking in the wind,
attached at the center,

and I wonder
how many worlds
could be saved
if more fathers
could be so dad-like.

II.

Tragedy

After the last fragment
of the hull has stopped bouncing
on the winter-hard brown
of a stubble-covered wheat field;

after the last flame
has surrendered to the blanket
of drizzle, applied like a salve
by sentient banks of clouds;

after the last plume of purple smoke
has been swept away by a flitting gust,
desperate to soften the glare
of the apocalyptic scene;

after the last suitcase,
gym bag, food tray, hand and
tennis shoe have been collected
into black plastic bags

and only the charred stalks,
craters, and trash of failed attempts
and lost intentions remain,

there comes that point, down the road,
when you grab your leg, lift
a foot from the wheelchair stirrup,
and touch the earth again.

There comes that point, eventually,
when you grab the rough bark
of the blackjack tree and pull
dead weight onto your legs.

And there even comes the point, hopefully,

when you lift the pen, pop off the lid
and force its tip down the faint,
familiar trail of paper that speaks
softly of your remembrance.

Broken

I'll write from the bottom,
stack letters and words—
maybe even enough punctuation—
around my feet at the base
of this dry well—
stepping up a layer at a time—
until piles of broken literature
raise my head to the surface.

There's little light down here.
But I only need a little—
enough to be able to read
the piles of broken literature
written by others.
To see how they got out—
what they did when they
got back to the surface.

Ashes to Dust

I sit on the outskirts
of the last few years
watching the artifices
of a previously peaceful,
somewhat directed, life
burn to the ground,
mostly smoke and ashes now,
the thunder of flames
reduced to a coughing
afterthought of
smoldering indictments
and popping epithets.

My forefinger quivers,
unconsciously scrapes
at an ashen smudge
on my forearm,
stirring up a quiet,
angelic laughter
at my amazing lapse
in understanding
the laws of heaven,
thinking I could make it
look clean again with enough
time and spit.

I soon leave it
in a sad gesture to remembrance,
and instead use the finger
to mark in the hard-baked sand—
a Messianic counting of sheep,
because shepherding may be
the only thing left to me
in the midst of this new,
Pacific-sized desert

descended from a warped
and brooding troposphere.

Not one of four geographic directions
offers a resurrected view.
So, I look back down and think
maybe I'll start with toes,
because toes
are most familiar
with the honesty
and demands
of dust.

Shattered

Help me, God!
Please…

I throw in a *Please* to soften
the demands of desperation.

Even though I'm not worth it,
he's always been great
with the not-worth-its.

Pull a great rescue here,
and I'll let it be known.

May not tell Oprah.
Doesn't seem your style.

But I'll tell the mice in my attic
and a few others that matter;
who listen with the ears mentioned
back in the gospels somewhere.

I Want to hear.
I want to get it.

That's where I am.
It's all I've got:

Shattered pieces of spirit heaped up
with a shovel of bare hands
bleeding from the sharp edges.

Firewalking

There's something about
knee-bending
moments—attacks
on the soul—that force
our noses to the gritty
floor and hold us there
until we wake up to that
pesky, incessant trope:
God is the last bastion.

There's something about
these red-eyed occasions—
a desperate pulse bulging
in our necks—that fling
an entire lifetime's baggage
out into Saturn's rings.

And when we survive, stand,
walk the luminous coals,
wade the Stygian void,
we find
a power
that throbs with life
and laughs
in the face of death.

Because, now we've seen
the phosphorescent center.

We no longer demand
cloud-written messages.

The next breath, next step
are signs enough.

Either Way
a note on postmodernism

There comes a point
when one chooses between
"something" and "nothing."

If one chooses nothing,
there's really no need
to waste any time
railing against those who
choose something.

No loss.
A lack of anything
requires no maintenance.

But, if there *is* something,
how can any one who
believes in nothing
blame the one who believes
in something
for proclaiming to the one
who believes in nothing
that there just might be
something
to this something-thing?

Test

I step into the flames.
Let the burn do its work.

My time with Christ
down in the under.

I breathe as best I can,
unafraid of my fear.

Hair singes away.
Skin turns to coal.

Must wait til it's done.
Then, I'll fall forward

and be dead, or
unstoppable.

Clutch

There's
something
about the very
bottom. Something
about not knowing if
you'll make it out alive.
There comes a point when
fear and pain   lose power,
   and you begin   to let go,
      realizing   the only thing
         left is to watch for what
            God will do in his timing.
            You release your grasp
               on dogma, and hope
                  grace will hold.

Behold, I Stand

My hand shakes—
not from caffeine.

I realize now
the only choice left

is to throw a bucket of
water at the gates of hell

and wait for the raging reply.
God, please, stand behind me.

Catch me. Hold up a hand
to defy Dante's flames,

then heal the melted holes
in my body and spirit.

Psalm before the Storm

The letter goes out tomorrow.
A letter that will incite anger,
rage, and lurid hatred.

Lord, allow a power
more powerful than mine;
a prayer more prayerful.

Hear the groans of angels,
language enough.

Sling your meteoric love
at this nightmare.

I'll give witness.

In Remission

Clouds of bats flap against
the insides of my skull.
I light candles and pray,
face to the floor,
for things C. S. Lewis told me
to be careful about; things
like the miracle of Juan Diego's
boy with the broken neck.

Like my friend Jim, on his knees,
praying about the mysterious,
black, they-only-know-about-
this-sort-of-thing-in-Houston
lump in his left triceps.

I need God to be touchy-feely,
big-hearted, big-handed—
heaven's own Coast Guard.

And all C. S. can tell me is:

gotta write poems anyway;
poems without answers;
poems right up to the moment
the black hood let's go
of the guillotine's rope.

Weak Defiance

When the news grows fangs...

When the doctor stares at the floor
        before he reads the diagnosis...

When the door swings open to the sunglasses
        of an unsmiling highway patrolman...

Before any words are uttered,
our minds fly away,
like sparrows when the back
door bangs the frame,
and we flutter off
to repaint the walls of hell,
to tidy it up for an early arrival.

In these capsized moments,
we run to the basement
of worst case scenarios.
It's as innate as drinking water.

This time, though, I will
swim against the great river—
choose the possibility of good.

The current is strong.
But my arms pound
the torrent of waves.
My feet search
for sand and rock.

A Wall for Wailing

I need a wall
this strong to lean
my life against.
Jerusalem stone,
yellowing in the scorch
of history, yet
mighty enough to stand
over millennia,
calming
the manic blur in my mind,
relaxing
the clenched fist of my spirit.

I have no proper hat,
no tassels or curls,
no Torah scroll or phylactery,
but I feel the hand
of something big
urging me forward anyway,
a heavenly breath
of acceptance and
permission,
a love
above the law.

III.

A Certain Darkness

He's a good kid.
I've never understood
good kids.

But he's a *really* good kid.

My eyes, normally able
to beam far into the recesses
behind outward appearances,
come up empty with him—
like watchin' the bobber
all afternoon, unaware the worm
fell off in the grass when casting.

He sits over there reading
his Bible, sipping chai,
making notes in a blank
journal.

On his way out,
he comes over to tell me
he's going to China
as a missionary.

He asks me how I'm doing,
like he almost really cares.
He's humble, confidently shy,
completely gorgeous—
a girl once told me.

There've been times before, though,
When I'd catch his eye
before he was ready,
and for a fraction of a second,
I saw the terror of some lie.

Coffeehouse Angels

I know now why people stop eating;
why Mindy rolls up in her sheets for days
at a time with the lights out, forearms
pressing thighs into chest, gently rocking.

I know why people stop washing their hair
one day without apparent reason;
why Glove Man, when he walks the streets,
wears multiple layers of clothing
against invisible fingers that extend out
from the little voices, causing him to swat
occasionally in the middle of sideways,
barely breathed soliloquies to tired angels
who have given up and sat down
in the dirt behind him.

I've begun to understand the silent language
the sunburned old lady mouths
at The Cup's back corner table—
an angel I've avoided until now,
hair like a neglected hound.

I may hold on to what she let go.
But I know now
why she did.

And the angels helped her do it.

Blowing Over

Religion has pulled her face down
and to the side a bit.
Eyes recede under the weight
of a brow that has so long born
concern for the lack of salvation
that surrounds her.

She still walks upright.
But her shoulders lead out first,
the rest of her body just a band
of frightened, obedient children
trying to keep a measured distance.

Like the half of the tree left standing
after the middle strike of the storm,
you know the next big wind...

In That Moment...

In the moment you turn
from the facts and evidence
on paper and take to staring
at the ceiling fan instead...

in the moment you relax fists
and lower arms in the face
of an oncoming punch...

in the moment words
cease to be the means
of rant and prayer...
in the moment victory
loses its appeal—
feels the same as defeat...

in that moment, you are ready
to live the beautiful life
that only comes from being
ready to die a beautiful death.

A Culinary Service

Is it possible to worship God
through every bite
of a breaded pork chop?

Does the light crunch
of a tiny yeast biscuit,
prepared by loving hands,
have spiritual significance?

Is chocolate one of
the forms of ambrosia—
a food of the gods
we're allowed to taste
through grace?

Is coffee the gritty
darkness sipped by angels
that keeps them from being gods?

Why

I write.
I want to be read,
heard in spite
of a million emails a minute,
and in spite
of a billion bubble jets spewing
half-lived dreams,
half-thought thoughts. And yet

I gasp in the bulge
of all that goes unsaid,
unwritten,
and the hope it undoes. So

I pray just one time,
maybe twice—
I'd take 21 if granted—
to write in the blood
of my fingers clawing
at the concrete of loss…

in the marrow of my bones
broken on a slab of devotion…

in the juices of my body
poured out in a sacrifice
for the sake of one who,
decades … centuries
beyond my death,
peels these pages,
unafraid to lick them
for a taste, a faint trace
of Golgotha's ink. Then

with an echo of Messianic

thunder still rolling
in the unquenchable distance,
she slams the book shut,
lights candles, pours wine,
folds back her own cover,
and dips a pen in the tears
of her own Gethsemane.

Resurrection

Phone rings at 8:59 a.m.
And before the second ring,
I relive the last three days
and two nights down below:

as my blood dripped
onto test slips, then—transcribed
into seven syllable words like
nucleic hieroglyphs on torch-lit
walls in my body— told
the myth of my life and death;

as I lit a Wal-Mart Virgencita
candle and spread pebbles
given me by my daughter, like
bones from a witch doctor's bag;

as I, deep in the entrails
of night, scratched the floor
in an effort to decode
divine communiqués
in the flick and bounce
of yellow flames;

as I never quite uttered
selfish prayers for redemption
and wholeness, paralyzed by
eleven million orphans in Africa;

then, as I woke this morning
to a heavy snowfall,
bowl of corn flakes and banana,
phone beside my hand, waiting…

Phone rings at 8:59 a.m.

Sixty seconds later,
I set it back down.

I turn my eyes to bright windows
and see the reprieve
signed in tears of angels
on a white blanket of grace
softly covering the barrenness
of a long relentless winter.

Misplaced Angel

Two uptown ladies, manicured,
pedicured, headicured, having
oatmeal with double-shot espressos.

One little girl, an angel separated
from the host, picks at a bagel.

Lady one sips, hopes the boys
of a friend straighten up soon
from the beer and pizza of fraternity;
hopes the girl of another friend
gets a good rush at sorority
so she'll find a good boy in fraternity.

Lady two swigs, drags through details
of the sordid difficulties of her life:
the lime green wallpaper
with a horrid floral pattern
that wallpaper man is redoing;
the barstools still in the back
of the 70s station wagon
of upholstery woman who
will not return calls.

Both swoon from disapproval,
shake heads at a disintegrating
world that no longer responds
properly to the whims and desires
of obvious superiority.

And the angel's eyes ping pong
with a dread they can't define,
and so, throw a prayer
across the small space between

clouds of Esteé Lauder base,
a prayer, a question, I worry
is prayed in my direction
because God is choking
on Dillard's dust:

"Will they return for me?"

The Anointing

I bumped the cup,
and a few drops
of coffee flopped over
its edge onto the title page
of Charles Bukowski's
Bone Palace Ballet.

After the reflex "Oh crap!"
I thought: *Wait,
it's Bukowski,
poet of barstools,
rats and roaches,
seedy motel rooms,*

and I drink his words
like a poison that kills
slowly enough not to matter
and realize

coffee stains
in this book
are nothing more,
yet nothing less
than a sprinkling
of Holy Water,

a silent nod to centuries
of withheld blessings
for prostitutes
and derelicts.

Eucharist

Breakfast with dad at Katy's
Cottage on Lincoln Avenue
in Carmel, California.

Talk over bread about books,
publishing, making a way
through the last half of life

by any path other than
the well-worn one
of the living dead.

In a night or two it'll be
dinner and wine with mom
at La Bohéme on Dolores Street.

Talk about painting and poetry,
necessary as air, water,
fire, and earth.

A few meals with mine,
God, as she sets about
her way in coming years;

a few conversations on dreams
and passion, and I promise
death will no longer be an issue.

My Four of Hearts

the line.

My heart holds love
like the numb, burned hands
of Hemingway's old man
gripping the rope
to the great fish
that murders him at sea.

the game.

My heart is a chessboard,
and I go through the motions
of the last few moves—
king one square to the right—
before the opponent attaches
"mate" to "check" and foregoes
the final take in honor of the defeated.

the storm.

My heart stands,
a lone Monterey Cypress,
thrashed and abused
by a century of Decembers
on the brooding California coast.

the statue.

My heart is the eye
Lot's wife turns behind her,
seeing the sulphuric fire,
then looking down to watch
the body turn to salt.

Foothold

I'd rather not believe my heart
is dead to love, having seen
one and one add up to
three or more once or twice. But

there's a roaring silence
my songs are given to…
nails me now and then
to trees, whatever's handy.

Christ's hell was enough for all,
but I feel the need to follow
him there on occasion
to resurrect lost intentions.

Poetic as it may seem
from a distance, it does nothing
to close the gaping chasm between
a potential friend and my self.

Still, the thought of a quiet toast
over foam and spray at sunset,
tears mingling with grapes,
sustains my longing for

love unafraid of loss
and separation, letting
its fields lie fallow
in shades of future growth.

The seed is a simple thing—
miracle that it remains.
It is a faith in the harvest
I must find my way back to.

The Private and the Poet

Private First Class.
Morris—US Army.
Shaved head, full fatigues,
and shin-high combat boots.

He pokes away at a chrome
Personal Digital Assistant
atop a black leather planner,
both full of what fuels him.

Two tables over, I sit—
greasy hair, 5 o'clock shadow,
frayed cargo shorts, Harvard
t-shirt, and black deck shoes.

I peck away at a sketchbook
with colored pens and whiteout.
Wendell Berry's Collected Poems
sit atop a paperback dictionary.

There was a time I would've shaken
my head at a young soldier's naïveté.
Now I see the foolishness
was altogether mine.

And though he may still shake his at me,
I say—God bless us both, the private
and the poet, our families, our dreams.
And save us from the pundit and the

president who tells the private
who to kill and ignores the poet's
protests of such historically blind,
delusional, ungodly commands.

Between Two Artists

Dear God,

        I have always admired
your work. And were it not for that,
I wouldn't bother you with this.

But I must say, your installation piece
at the Point Lobos Nature Reserve
above Big Sur simply goes too far.

The Monterey Pines are too tall,
the Cypresses too fanned out
in perfection from trunks tied
in intricate knots that would take
centuries to unravel.

                The cliffs appear
superimposed for dramatic effect
with impossible jags giving way
to fairytale caves that burst forth
gushes of blue water like a French soda
topped with cotton candy cream spray.

The crash of waves and explosions of foam
are too much like a Disney Land ride.
There are too many kinds of birds, too many
varieties of plants, and too much color in both.

In short, it lacks integrity. It does not speak
to the truth of the way things are. And I don't
think viewers will trust or believe its authenticity.

Too Much Information

I saw
God
tonight.

What I Mean Is...

I have come to believe
the modern machine
of conservative Christianity
is very little more
than a complete, utter
breakdown of etymology.
We're awash in a mad sea of
misunderstanding, misrepresentation,
misinterpretation and misusage by
a few high profile, misanthropic,
misogynistic misfits.

The More Things Change…

A tramp, hussy, she'd be called
if not for the recent
wave of political correctness.

She sits at a table with friends
on the coffee shop patio—
tousled, unwashed hair,
steely eyes of the street,
succulent, mud-brown limbs,
ember of cigarette flashing
across a small factory
of cheap silver jewelry.

A local gray-haired pastor
walking by on his way
back to church
steals a lengthy glance
at her tan breasts
heaving with laughter
and poetic license.

To My Surprise

It seems after a while
we'd give up any and all
shock
at the human capacity
for mind-bending badness—
infanticide, the holocaust,
a mother pulling up in front
of Grandma's one day
with the new boyfriend
and dropping the kids off,
permanently.

Then again,
maybe that's the key to the lock
evil conceals in deep shadows:
Remain surprised.

Let the surges and jolts
of war and rape
snap the wires of sensibility
like a May tornado in Oklahoma.

Then jump up, if you can,
and stare the source in its face,
raise an arm with an extended
forefinger at the end,
and let the badness
know
                    that you know.

Wha' da ya do?

Coupla minister friends
meet me at the Cup
on Wednesdays—
deep-fried heretics both.

We bitch and moan
and sling crap at Christians
and other ministers we think
must starch their bras and boxers.

We talk about leaving
the ministry so we could
finally minister in some way
that might matter.

Just like we talk about
spiking our coffee with kalua
and Irish cream in broad
daylight, but never do.

We pause to listen to a drunk
taxi driver and college prof
trade profanities about the war,
then scratch our water glasses

right before heading out to our
respective missions committee meetings.

IV.

Losin' It

God's gone mad.
'Course
how can you blame 'im?
Think about it—
you sink a few million,
or, ten thousand years—
[whichever you wanna believe]
into this creation project
and then, on the eighth day
your crowning achievement
sells itself down a shit river
of McDonalds and Wal-Marts.

We sent in a team of psychologists,
but he refused medication, laughing:
What the hell are you talking about?
I invented fucked-up. You know?
For color. But I never intended
for everyone to hook up with it.

We sent in a team of ministers,
but that *really* pissed 'im off.
Before they even got a chance
to whip out a tract and remind
the Lord of all Creation of his
Four Spiritual Laws, he shot off:
Look! I cut off communication
with you jackasses over 1800
years ago, and I'm not about
to start it back up again
with the black hole you've created,
sucking all the spiritual light
out of my universe.

We still see 'im now and then
among the rocks and trees,
walking along the shore at night,
puffin' on a Swisher Sweet.

Makes No Sense

Even with the invisible anvils time
has tied to my neck and shoulders,
I smile more than I used to, raise
my head skyward and laugh with God.

Even with all the pennies lost
down the drain, the occasional
minor fortunes washed away
in a flood of bad decisions,
I am more grateful than I used to be.
I cherish each minute awarded
like a quarter's-worth of time
on the mechanical horse in front
of the old grocery store.

Even though people are worse
than I had initially suspected
as a young man—full of crap
beyond imagination—I love them
more than ever, want to play
in their lives like a pony in the edges
of a pond, occasionally stopping
to take a long deep drink.

Makeover

They've pulled him from the cross,
Brooks Brothered him out in a deep
navy suit with a maroon tie
and some nice leather Cole Haans.

When he tries to step into the synagogue
for prayer, they grab his elbow and suggest,
Uhh… we don't go there anymore. We have these
nice new buildings out on the interstate. Much
more conducive to larger P.A. systems, bigger
offerings, and live television feeds, you understand.

He makes a dash for the tomb in hopes
of a few days rest, but they won't have it.
No time. Service starts at eleven hundred
hours, so hell will have to wait.

We're on air in five… and the techs
flip on the spotlights, blinding him
before he can raise his forearms in front
of his eyes, and only because he's God
does he understand the way in which
his image is beamed to a satellite
and then turned back towards earth
in a spray that reminds him of the
original rejection. He almost smiles
at this protestant stab at transubstantiation.

After the service—that leaves him
feeling unheard once again—some
of the wealthier members want to
take him to lunch at the Oak Tree
Country Club. He would prefer
a quiet hillside for some meditation,

but they recommend Mondays as being
better for that and warn him to watch
his head as he ducks into the back seat
of the black stretch limo.

The pastor asks if he'd like to come over
and check out the Cowboys on FOX
or just head back to the Marriot for a nap.

And that's when Jesus breaks at a dead run
for the pond on the eighteenth hole
and wades out as far as he can,
because there is no boat this time,
because there are no fishermen
this time, and so he drops his face
into his hands, weeping uncontrollably.

Finding Jesus

First Baptist Church—my shoulders jerk up
when the new preacher's spit hits my cheek.

Folks! Jesus is comin' again!
And it could be any minute now!
Just look at the sins of this world!

So, during the next tear-soaked prayer,
I slip out the back door to wait for him—
eyes scanning the sidewalks, I wonder
what he'll look like this time.

Impatience takes me across Webster St.
to the First Christian Church. I look
for him there. Nothin' doin'.

From there, I walk a block over
to University Blvd. and find no Savior
around McFarland Methodist either.

As a last ditch effort, I head south
on University to First Presbyterian
and catch my breath for a second
when I spot a homeless man on a bench
in the shade. Not Him, but the closest
thing I've seen this morning. I ask
if he's seen any heavenly beings. He raises
a brown paper bag and slobbers
a profoundly quiet, "Yesss…"

He offers nothing more, so
I shrug it off and slide down
the back alley to Campus Corner.
The Korean-owned Sunshine Store is open.

I buy a longneck and sink down
by the payphone out in front.

Half way through the bottle, some guy
in camo pants and a sleeveless black
T-shirt squats down next to me.
He asks for a sip.

Sure... I say, staring
at the pavement.
He's respectfully quiet.

So, it's a minute or two
before I recognize him.

Dead Heretics Society

I've filled my home
with sinners.
Frisbee players
and Lutherans.
Gnostic engineers.
Mormon environmentalists
and a returned Baptist missionary
for color—more color
than Zaccheus could have dreamed
possible at his little party.
I've even thrown in
a lawyer and a tax collector
for biblical soundness.
All here for the poker
and little smokies with a Bud.
All in preparation
for the Savior's return.

Peace in the Middle West

My friend sees God in an ankle-length
white robe with glasses and gray hair,
nose scrunched in a "hmm" of concern
over all the ink on your life's page.

I see a paint-splattered smock
and unkempt hair, a brush paused
above canvas as he re-imagines all
possible histories for a present future.

My friend sees books in Greek and Hebrew
with footnotes in fat concordances.
I feel the Braille of rocks and fish
and angels blowing up pumpkin balloons.

And we simply do not agree as we
annie-up between sips of Honey Brown,
each trying to read the cards in the other's
eyes, laughing, taking turns losing, and…

no Hitlers sprout from a pair of aces,
no babies die in a straight flush of clubs,
no families are shelled out of a full house
in our war fought with poker chips
and one-eyed jacks.

Yap!

I'm afraid God
may not be religious.

Matter of fact, the further
I get from religion's fiery core,
the more it looks like a little
angry dog yanking on
the pant leg of divinity—

divinity leaning over, speaking
gently, trying to help, but
the little dog doesn't understand
divinity's language, and so

it just yelps and barks,
and it ain't ever gonna learn
to sit or heel. It just yaps
incessantly ... cause ...
that's what little yappy dogs do.

I Have My Reasons

A lack of discretion over class,
race and gender was the reason
Jesus was always leaving
wherever he had just been.

An outright disrespect
for chains of command
was the reason he was
hunted like a boar.

But it was staring into the faces
of high priests and telling them
they were losing their minds,
that got him killed.

And all these together are
the reasons I will not lose sleep
over any slobbering rants
against these poems.

A Single God

                   The guy keeps talkin'
like the Son of God's celibacy
was a given—a must—as if Jesus
couldn't have loved a woman
like my father loved my mother
for fifty years; as if it would've
ruined heaven's whole shebang.

                        And I,
with all respect and gratitude
to my parents, think about last night:

the burger at Don's Alley, bike ride
to the movies, cup o' Milano
Espresso at the café afterwards
with the Fat Fall Publisher's Weekly,
then the purchase of John Mayer's
latest album, the ride back to the car,
sunroof rolled back, windows
down, driving for no other reason
than the new CD, head tilted back
watching streetlights flash by,
draggin' the entire length of Main
goin', the length of Lindsay comin'
back, 66 degrees, and John's
tellin' me there's a girl that
puts the color inside o' my world.
But they can't quite get it together
because of somethin' in her childhood.

Then I think *Yup. That's it.*
Evenings like this. Girls like that.
That's why Jesus stayed single, man.
It wasn't some holy, high-brow,

heaven-keepin'-up-appearances
kind o' thing.

It was because he was omniscient.

Two Little Words

Apparently, we owe it to a baker somewhere,
in or around 1620, who put the words
"one" and "way" together to label
a kind of bread eaten with oysters
before the meale... *one way bread.*

I'm curious what the ingredients were.
Because somewhere between the grating
teeth of the next few centuries, the words
"one-way" grew into two three-headed dragons
chained together, spewing fire, wreaking holy havoc.

These two little words set crazies like
Alexander Inglis and James Bryant Conant
off on a turn of the 20th century warpath
thinking the straight-legged, knee-
high boot-stomping educational system
of the Prussians would be a good thing
for our children; make for the best soldiers,
floor-moppers and assembly-line workers—
heads in permanent bow to wealth.

These two words licensed the delusional
alchemy of Southern Baptists to infuse
the Bible with veins and arteries—
give it Frankenstein's heart pumping
with the blood of Dixie; sew on the
arms and legs of orthodoxy and cram
the brain of Judas into it's skull—
a total eclipse of Christ.

And these two words make it impossible
for a president to admit mistakes, a secretary
of defense to plead temporary insanity,

and for both to step back from the boiling
cauldron of far away nations with the eyeballs
and the hands of children floating in it.

Elusive

The center of the Milky Way's
swirl   be   it
made of stars   or
c a r a m e l and white chocolate
is the eye of my
                  self
searching what lies just beyond
what is known
                  for some new
candy   hidden
        by God
in the lumpy folds of dark space

                  heaven's pantry.

On the Way

Dad's retired and on his way
to pinch-hit preach in Tulsa
on an October Sunday morning.

He has a certain coffee stop
just before the turnpike,
a favorite form of meditation.

He pulls up to the window and
reaches for the football-shaped,
rubber coin purse in his pocket

that I remember playing with
when I was five, or so.
She leans out, "Mornin'.

You all dressed up.
On your way to church?"
"Well, actually, I'm on my way

to Tulsa to preach this morning."
"Oh! So you a pastor." "Yes."
"Well… would you pray

for me right now? I got some
negative people and thoughts
in my life I needa get rid of."

Dad says sure, then she asks
for his hand. He reaches up.
He prays.   She squeezes.

And I imagine myself into
the car in line just behind him
seeing the white hand extended

from the cuff of a white shirt
clasped by the two beautiful
black hands at the ends of a gray

uniform and wonder if the sight
alone would be enough to bow
my head in worship with them.

Bad

Sometimes
I just run out.
Out of steam.
And I get tired of being good.
I yell at a friend on the Frisbee field.
Get surprisingly angry. It's been a day now.
And I still don't care to apologize. Not sure I care
if I see him again. Because I'm just tired. I want to be bad.
Good wears me out. And nothing wears me out more than terminally good people. Ned Flanders types. Life bitch-slaps 'em into a smelly dumpster full of rusty razor blades, and they pop out bleeding and praising Jesus. I mean, even Jesus appears to have had his off moments. People drove him nuts at the same time he loved them enough to die for them. I recall a whip of ropes and flying tables—one of the great Gospel moments that helps me believe in him more. Like a bad Mel Gibson movie, we're all thinkin' it— "Yeah! Give it to 'em, Jesus! Those hoity-toity, cheatin' bastards."

Taking It Back

the poem I suppose
I would have written begins:
it's still shocking, even though
you know it's coming,
to witness so first-hand
the death of a church,
like being present at the
break and slide of glacier
into ocean. Eleven or twelve
people sit, look uncomfortably
at all the empty metal chairs while
the preacher speaks in a tone
and at a volume more appropriate
for hundreds, to these few remaining
like the rich folks on the Titanic
who sat there patiently, because
the wealthy simply do not drown. But,

then came the responsive reading
of the Prayer of Confession, voices
out of tempo, and my tired,
limping life rose to the surface
like a cautious whale, spewing
the scatter of scripture up into my face.

The words were for me,
and I had to take them,
accept them, let the tear form

and rewrite the poem.

Rest for Angels

When I left Norman before sunrise
the temperature was in the mid-sixties.
After sunset here in Manitou Springs
I draw in the elixir of thirty-one degrees.

Once again, I am in the one-man
booth in the far back corner
of the Twelve Tribe's café reading
and writing poetry by the yellow bulb.

Once again, I feel my breath slow down
just behind the bridge of my nose.
And I know the angels assigned
to hold together my fractured mind—
administer my daily doses of grace
and pardon—have sat down by
the chilly springs just out the window
to rest and talk about other things
for a while.

V.

Verb Play

When I'm forced to spend time around zealous minister types, I keep hearing about the necessity of reaching out to the "unchurched." The obvious implication being: we need to "church" the "unchurched."

Now, this particular verbish usage of the word "unchurch" does not appear in my fairly large dictionary. What I do see is the transitive verb that means to excommunicate. This definition is clearer to me. And it helps me organize my response:

Dear friends,
    our deepest need is not to "church" the "unchurched," but to "dechurch" the "enchurched"—that is to say, the excessively "churched."

> *God Save Me from Your Followers*

has ceased to be a humorous bumper sticker. It is now a genuine fear for many of the "unchurched" to which you refer.

And as we look for solutions, a good place to start would be to "depolitic" "enchurched" leaders. But, in the end, [and while we're in the practice of verbing up nouns] nothing—and I reiterate—nothing supercedes the desperate need for Christians to "reJesus" the church.

A Faith Between

I'm trying to decide what I believe in
anymore. And I begin with consideration
of what I don't believe in anymore:

I don't believe in hell anymore as some
sort of Club Dead hidden on the coast
of Baja California where the hot tubs

boil instead of bubble and the ocean
breaks with waves of molten lava—
where massages are given with pumice

stones, and cocktails of liquid silver
with little lead umbrellas come with
an hors d' oeuvre of live sand crabs.

And if I still believe in heaven,
it is in the sense that I'm certain
I've been there without dying—

meaning, I think it's open for business,
but we've lost the map and don't wanna
drive over to the "other side" to look for it

anymore. It's just that my ex-wife called
a few minutes ago, and they've taken a
look at the x-rays, and they're afraid

my little girl's got pneumonia, and so
I'm rummaging through my backpack,
because there's something I've lost,
and I really, really need to find it.

on Saving the World

It's a loose arrangement of misfits that show up at my little house on Monday nights. We eat, watch South Park, play poker sometimes, but then, always, sink into deep philosophical sword-play with words.

It began, years ago, with me warming up frozen corndog nuggets and taquitos while I set out a two liter Coke, Dr. Pepper, and Sprite. It culminated last night into frying up thick sliced ham, cooking scrambled eggs in the grease, then making homemade biscuits, cranberry sauce, pumpkin spice cake with rum sauce, and my own special recipe for sangria. And this is while Denae is unwrapping her garlic cheese bread and Charley is popping the cork on German Riesling and mixing caramel apple martinis.

We sit cross-legged on carpet, plates and glasses strewn about, and go at it on judging not, lest ye be judged. Some of them feel my writings are rather judgmental. And I'd say they're fairly justified in judging me as such. And Chad and I go at it pretty heavily, and no one thinks a thing of it, including the two of us. Everyone chimes in. Time does its thing like a glassy-eyed creek. And the fire is now nothing but coals, and we're all laughing, and Chad and I hug. And we talk about stars, Christmas lights, how cold it is through clouds of breath as I walk them out to cars and shared rides. I come back in and wash dishes.

I dream all night about getting in trouble at church for bringing food into the auditorium, playing the wrong tune on the wrong instrument, laughing at inappropriate times. I'm a preteen. Angry women are throwing hands up in the air. Suit-clad men come in to deal with me. And I am telling them all about the early church, how they gathered loosely at someone's house, probably ate together, and probably fought over the heavenly wealth of information that the Son of God had recently dumped on them. And how they tried to stay together around the central theme of love.

And I went on to tell them how they'd missed the whole damn boat and needed to strip those ridiculous clothes off and start swimming.

I awoke to early morning sun and thoughts of how we've taught children that church services are about boredom and expensive shoes. How we've taught teenagers that it's about finding the best spot in the back. And that when we leave the service and step outside, we get a clear picture of the fact that it's also about expensive, big-ass cars. You've gotta throw in a healthy dose of fear—without which very few people would remain. And how we've taken the holy scriptures and turned them into what Reverend Lovejoy on the Simpsons refers to as a "two-thousand page sleeping pill."

I rub some of the sleep from my eyes, yawn, and sit up into a cloud of revelation:

I recall the few times my daughter has been at these meetings. I ponder the way she sat petting Wenda, Denae's service-dog-in-training, and was *riveted* to our conversations. You could see little wheels turning. You could see churning and amazement. And she loves the food. And she loves these people. She calls them the "big kids." And she never wants to go to bed. She falls asleep of attrition on the floor, or in someone's lap, because—

something's going on here,
and she knows it.

That's when I realize—this is it—what could quite possibly save the world—just what Chad and I did last night—eat, hit the *big stuff*, go at it, fight a little, disagree, stretch, hold on, and then...

hug.

Roman Holiday

I have to pass by the mall
every day—every day
I decide to get out, that is.

And I go in there, I guess,
once a year, whether I need to
or not—usually for choco-beans.

But this annual visit will *never*,
by the hair of my chinny-chin-chin,
fall on the day after Thanksgiving.

On this holiest of holy days
the edifices of commerce morph
into neo-Roman coliseums.

Driving by, a few minutes before
opening, I see that every parking slot
is filled with shining idle horses.

Gladiators stand beside them buckling
on their body armor, sliding checkbooks
into holsters, extra wallets into boots.

And I, in my deep love for irony,
cannot hide my affection for how
it's all for the sake of Christ's mass,

and that in every logoed shopping bag
are carried all the bits and pieces
of the antithesis of his message.

It's Sunday in America

and somewhere, in some church, in every town, in every state,
some preacher, "speaker," is scaring the hell out of people—in the
love of Christ, of course. There are few things in the universe this
constant, this reliable.

They're tellin' us how it's gonna be… how it's all gonna go
down. Who's turnin'. Who's burnin'. And *why*! And sometimes I
wanna go find Harvey [the guy whose holy advert I just read].
Track him down. Sit in the audience and at an opportune time
shout out "Hey Harve! Whaduya think about fags? Whaduya think
about Negras n' them women who wanna speak their peace …
even *preach* for God's sake?"

But not really. Because I know the answers. I know because of
the shape and slight amber tint to his glasses. I know because of
the pubic symbolism in his moustache. I know because he calls
himself a "speaker" instead of a preacher.

And I think about the title of his revival-go-t'-meetin'

"Earth: Taken Hostage!"

And I think "Damn straight!" And I think a better use of my
time would be to go sit on the curb out front with Jesus and put
my arm around him while he cries…

again.

Sunday School

Cain swoops in to Sunday school
on the wings of pterodactyls,
a virginal sip of blood and murder
for wide-eyed first grade Abels.

Sugared truth sprinkles youth
from scripture playing twister
in the scary words of an insecure
spitting and shrieking pastor.

"Wait!" I scream, at what seem
such empty wooden faces.
But no one listens to words not spoken
From the holy, pulpity places.

Lost in Spaces

I see holiday visions through the window
that frames the space between Thanksgiving
and Christmas. It's the slice of year
where the heaven-held knife slurps up
all the extra frosting, not wanting to waste it.

My toes are cold from taking the table
on the north wall of the Red Cup.
I wrap my fingers around hot porcelain.
Blues on the stereo remind me
of the merits of discomfort. And I sit
inside the warmth of gratitude for the quiet
vacancies shoppers leave in the wake
of their maniacal urges and misplaced love
in search of a ticket to forgiveness.

In Fusion

I'm beginning to understand why so many
older people are quiet in the mix of family
and social gatherings, the back row in big church,
or the picnic that follows. What I once thought
a lack of liveliness, I now see as patience.

They softly suffer through our absolutes,
truths we're so sure are roasted to perfection.
They listen to the college punk in the pulpit
and smile at an ignorance they survived,
remembering how it burned in the flames of failure.

And I, a teacher between generations,
field questions of "What's it all about?"
and have only learned enough to point to the back
where seasoned lips wait to speak what tender
ears must wait to hear, and I stand there
in the middle stretching for a hand of each,
hoping I won't blow like a low amp fuse
in the surge of power when the circuit completes.

Long Lay the World

I perform a few songs in the midnight
Christmas Eve service every year.
Don't think I've missed in a decade.
It's a soft hour. A meaningful time. Yet,

I've managed to turn it into work. Something
I've gotta do. Religion's desperation rakes
fingernails across the letters of scriptures
on the chalkboard to the point I've lost all focus.

But in the back hallway retuning my guitar
between songs, I see a police car fly by
on Main. Guns and knives don't take holidays.
I feel a metaphor slice into my lagging heart.

I go back out to close with O Holy Night,
to look like my mind's on manger scenes,
and instead, pray a silent prayer of peace
for the endless work of uniforms and badges.

Heartland Hippie

So I have to speak to the 7th
through 12th graders at this moderate
church tomorrow morning, liberal,
by Oklahoma standards, I suppose.

And I've forgotten what people
that age think about, care about
besides game controllers and Grand
Theft Auto. But the real problem

is all my liberated hippie friends
in the coffee shop right now, glancing
nervously at my table while I rifle
through my NAS Master Study Bible

looking for 2nd Chronicles where
Solomon prays for wisdom instead
of wealth, and because he did, gets
both anyway. And I want to tell

the hippies, "Look, at least I'm doin'
Solomon, the biggest screw-up in the
Bible. Except maybe for his dad. Oh yeah,
and that co-dependent loser, Hosea."

Bound for Paradise

Who else does that—
declares a
Day of Rage?

Now, dadgummit, I am
a flaming liberal-hippie-type,
and I'm supposed to love

everyone—except maybe CEOs.
I'm supposed to sympathize
with the Palestinians, but then

they go and actually set aside
a day devoted to hate and rage.
That's all they're going to do

outside of maybe some dinner
around seven or eight o'clock.
They're going to rage against Jews

and Israelis, American capitalist
dogs, oh, and don't forget the British
who snuck off in '48 and left them

in this mess. Now, the Jews
have the "Days of Awe," and
Daytona has its "Days of Thunder,"

and the Cherokees have memories
of the "Trail of Tears," but this?
this legacy to grandchildren?

Yes, Punkin, those were the days,
The Days of Rage. We poured
into the streets and hated people.

Leap Night

February 29

I'm in a small worship service
on a Sunday evening. They asked
me to read a few of my poems.

I feel like a black man in a hood
and gloves at a Ku Klux Klan
meeting in Rogers, Arkansas.

And if they rip my hood off—
open my book and read the poems
I'm so carefully avoiding tonight—

These fine folks will lynch me
in the few beats of their hearts
it takes to leap from there to here.

Movie Review

I knew how it ended.
But I went anyway—
against what I thought
was my better judgment.

Hollywood pokes its finger
into religion's pie again, and
the people's passions ignite
in a far less finely tuned way

than the original Passion
of the Christ himself.
We hate the violence, or
think it necessary. We're

glad about Mel or mad
as hell about Mel. And
my friend hated it with a
passion. So, I loved it.

Song of Imperfection

I sing the song of imperfection
the song of Bly's retarded children
forgotten in their bleeding nation

I sing the ode of Lincoln's sadness
Tchaikovsky's, sweet with madness
the good inside such biblical badness

I sing the hymn of rotting crosses
all Jerusalem's wins and losses
the storm of history's turns and tosses

and contemplate Jesus throwing tables.

Half

In dreams of hope and blood
I place a rusty bucket below my soul's
leaky faucet to catch the drip of words
that wage attrition's war on my mind.

Sometimes, when it looks half empty,
I throw it out the back door
believing it will nourish
beauty of a more wordless nature.

Other times, when it appears half full,
I dash it onto a canvas,
stand over it for hours, days,
head cocked to the right, then left,

believing...

believing that even half
of all this crazy world's
hopeful and bloody dreams
could mean the difference.